Booked
& Busy

ROMANCE READING JOURNAL

BOOKED AND BUSY ROMANCE READING JOURNAL

© Copyright 2025 Publish Her Press

ISBN: 978-1-962457-55-2 (Softcover)

Printed in the United States of America

Published by Publish Her, LLC
6726 Walker Street
St. Louis Park, MN 55426
www.publishherpress.com

Publish Her is a female-founded publisher dedicated to
educating authors and elevating the words, stories
and writing of women.

PUBLISH **HER**™

HOW TO USE THIS JOURNAL

Track and organize the romance books you read and record your thoughts in this specialty journal for booklovers. It's designed to be used with or without a mini printer (not included).

The front pages of this journal serve as a book tracker. List the books you read, the authors, and the page numbers that correspond to your journal entries, so you can quickly refer to them later.

Next, you'll find guided journaling pages. They include space for cover art, which you can print and paste into your journal. Or doodle your own! Prompts help you rate characters, plot, writing and the overall book, with dedicated space for your reviews. There's also room to note highlights, quotes and questions.

This journal is designed to fit in your purse, backpack or tote bag, so you can easily jot down notes on the go. Keep it with you to share your thoughts during bookish conversations with friends or discussions with book club members.

It's a lasting keepsake to help you remember your favorite books and what you loved most about them.

ROMANCE BOOK TRACKER

Pages	
2-3	Book Title _____ Author _____
Pages	
4-5	Book Title _____ Author _____
Pages	
6-7	Book Title _____ Author _____
Pages	
8-9	Book Title _____ Author _____
Pages	
10-11	Book Title _____ Author _____
Pages	
12-13	Book Title _____ Author _____
Pages	
14-15	Book Title _____ Author _____
Pages	
16-17	Book Title _____ Author _____
Pages	
18-19	Book Title _____ Author _____
Pages	
20-21	Book Title _____ Author _____

Pages	Book Title
22–23	Author

Pages	Book Title
24–25	Author

Pages	Book Title
26–27	Author

Pages	Book Title
28–29	Author

Pages	Book Title
30–31	Author

Pages	Book Title
32–33	Author

Pages	Book Title
34–35	Author

Pages	Book Title
36–37	Author

Pages	Book Title
38–39	Author

Pages	Book Title
40–41	Author

Pages	Book Title _____
42-43	Author _____

Pages	Book Title _____
44-45	Author _____

Pages	Book Title _____
46-47	Author _____

Pages	Book Title _____
48-49	Author _____

Pages	Book Title _____
50-51	Author _____

Pages	Book Title _____
52-53	Author _____

Pages	Book Title _____
54-55	Author _____

Pages	Book Title _____
56-57	Author _____

Pages	Book Title _____
58-59	Author _____

Pages	Book Title _____
60-61	Author _____

Pages	Book Title
62-63	Author

Pages	Book Title
64-65	Author

Pages	Book Title
66-67	Author

Pages	Book Title
68-69	Author

Pages	Book Title
70-71	Author

Pages	Book Title
72-73	Author

Pages	Book Title
74-75	Author

Pages	Book Title
76-77	Author

Pages	Book Title
78-79	Author

Pages	Book Title
80-81	Author

Pages	Book Title _____
82–83	Author _____

Pages	Book Title _____
84–85	Author _____

Pages	Book Title _____
86–87	Author _____

Pages	Book Title _____
88–89	Author _____

Pages	Book Title _____
90–91	Author _____

Pages	Book Title _____
92–93	Author _____

Pages	Book Title _____
94–95	Author _____

Pages	Book Title _____
96–97	Author _____

Pages	Book Title _____
98–99	Author _____

Pages	Book Title _____
100–101	Author _____

Pages	Book Title _____
102–103	Author _____

Pages	Book Title _____
104–105	Author _____

Pages	Book Title _____
106–107	Author _____

Pages	Book Title _____
108–109	Author _____

Pages	Book Title _____
110–111	Author _____

Pages	Book Title _____
112–113	Author _____

Pages	Book Title _____
114–115	Author _____

Pages	Book Title _____
116–117	Author _____

Pages	Book Title _____
118–119	Author _____

Pages	Book Title _____
120–121	Author _____

Pages	Book Title _____
122–123	Author _____

Pages	Book Title _____
124–125	Author _____

Pages	Book Title _____
126–127	Author _____

Pages	Book Title _____
128–129	Author _____

Pages	Book Title _____
130–131	Author _____

Pages	Book Title _____
132–133	Author _____

Pages	Book Title _____
134–135	Author _____

Pages	Book Title _____
136–137	Author _____

Pages	Book Title _____
138–139	Author _____

Pages	Book Title _____
140–141	Author _____

Pages	Book Title _____
142–143	Author _____

Pages	Book Title _____
144–145	Author _____

Pages	Book Title _____
146–147	Author _____

Pages	Book Title _____
148–149	Author _____

Pages	Book Title _____
150–151	Author _____

Pages	Book Title _____
152–153	Author _____

Pages	Book Title _____
154–155	Author _____

Pages	Book Title _____
156–157	Author _____

Pages	Book Title _____
158–159	Author _____

Pages	Book Title _____
160–161	Author _____

Pages	Book Title _____
162-163	Author _____

Pages	Book Title _____
164-165	Author _____

Pages	Book Title _____
166-167	Author _____

Pages	Book Title _____
168-169	Author _____

Pages	Book Title _____
170-171	Author _____

Pages	Book Title _____
172-173	Author _____

Pages	Book Title _____
174-175	Author _____

Pages	Book Title _____
176-177	Author _____

Pages	Book Title _____
178-179	Author _____

Pages	Book Title _____
180-181	Author _____

Pages	Book Title _____
182–183	Author _____
Pages	Book Title _____
184–185	Author _____
Pages	Book Title _____
186–187	Author _____
Pages	Book Title _____
188–189	Author _____
Pages	Book Title _____
190–191	Author _____
Pages	Book Title _____
192–193	Author _____
Pages	Book Title _____
194–195	Author _____
Pages	Book Title _____
196–197	Author _____
Pages	Book Title _____
198–199	Author _____
Pages	Book Title _____
200–201	Author _____

ROMANCE READING JOURNAL

Book Title and Author or Cover Art	Spice Level 🌶🌶🌶🌶🌶

Format _____

Number of Pages _____

Date Started _____

Date Finished _____

Recommend _____

_____

_____

Characters	Plot	Writing	Overall
☆☆☆☆☆	☆☆☆☆☆	☆☆☆☆☆	☆☆☆☆☆

Review _____

_____

_____

_____

_____

_____

_____

_____

_____

_____

_____

_____

_____

Highlights and Quotes _____

_____

_____

_____

_____

_____

_____

_____

Questions _____

_____

_____

_____

_____

_____

_____

Playlist _____

_____

_____

_____

_____

_____

Book Title and Author or Cover Art	Spice Level 🌶🌶🌶🌶🌶

Spice Level 🌶🌶🌶🌶🌶

Format _____

Number of Pages _____

Date Started _____

Date Finished _____

Recommend _____

_____

_____

Characters	Plot	Writing	Overall
☆☆☆☆☆	☆☆☆☆☆	☆☆☆☆☆	☆☆☆☆☆

Review _____

_____

_____

_____

_____

_____

_____

_____

_____

_____

_____

_____

Highlights and Quotes _____

_____

_____

_____

_____

_____

_____

Questions _____

_____

_____

_____

_____

_____

Playlist _____

_____

_____

_____

_____

_____

Book Title and Author or Cover Art	Spice Level 🌶🌶🌶🌶🌶
	Format _____
	Number of Pages _____
	Date Started _____
	Date Finished _____
	Recommend _____
	_____
	_____

Characters	Plot	Writing	Overall
☆☆☆☆☆	☆☆☆☆☆	☆☆☆☆☆	☆☆☆☆☆

Review _____

_____

_____

_____

_____

_____

_____

_____

_____

_____

_____

_____

Highlights and Quotes _____

_____

_____

_____

_____

_____

_____

_____

Questions _____

_____

_____

_____

_____

_____

_____

Playlist _____

_____

_____

_____

_____

_____

_____

Book Title and Author or Cover Art	Spice Level 🌶🌶🌶🌶🌶

Format _____

Number of Pages _____

Date Started _____

Date Finished _____

Recommend _____

_____

_____

Characters	Plot	Writing	Overall
☆☆☆☆☆	☆☆☆☆☆	☆☆☆☆☆	☆☆☆☆☆

Review _____

_____

_____

_____

_____

_____

_____

_____

_____

_____

_____

_____

Highlights and Quotes _____

_____

_____

_____

_____

_____

_____

Questions _____

_____

_____

_____

_____

_____

Playlist _____

_____

_____

_____

_____

_____

Book Title and Author or Cover Art	Spice Level 🌶🌶🌶🌶🌶

Format _____

Number of Pages _____

Date Started _____

Date Finished _____

Recommend _____

_____

_____

Characters	Plot	Writing	Overall
☆☆☆☆☆	☆☆☆☆☆	☆☆☆☆☆	☆☆☆☆☆

Review _____

_____

_____

_____

_____

_____

_____

_____

_____

_____

_____

_____

Highlights and Quotes _____

_____

_____

_____

_____

_____

_____

_____

Questions _____

_____

_____

_____

_____

_____

_____

Playlist _____

_____

_____

_____

_____

_____

_____

Book Title and Author or Cover Art	Spice Level 🌶🌶🌶🌶🌶

Format _____

Number of Pages _____

Date Started _____

Date Finished _____

Recommend _____

_____

_____

Characters	Plot	Writing	Overall
☆☆☆☆☆	☆☆☆☆☆	☆☆☆☆☆	☆☆☆☆☆

Review _____

_____

_____

_____

_____

_____

_____

_____

_____

_____

_____

_____

_____

Highlights and Quotes _____

_____

_____

_____

_____

_____

_____

_____

Questions _____

_____

_____

_____

_____

_____

_____

Playlist _____

_____

_____

_____

_____

_____

Book Title and Author or Cover Art	Spice Level 🌶🌶🌶🌶🌶

Format _____

Number of Pages _____

Date Started _____

Date Finished _____

Recommend _____

_____

_____

Characters	Plot	Writing	Overall
☆☆☆☆☆	☆☆☆☆☆	☆☆☆☆☆	☆☆☆☆☆

Review _____

_____

_____

_____

_____

_____

_____

_____

_____

_____

_____

Highlights and Quotes _____

_____

_____

_____

_____

_____

_____

Questions _____

_____

_____

_____

_____

_____

Playlist _____

_____

_____

_____

_____

_____

Book Title and Author or Cover Art	Spice Level 🌶🌶🌶🌶🌶

Format _____

Number of Pages _____

Date Started _____

Date Finished _____

Recommend _____

_____

_____

Characters	Plot	Writing	Overall
☆☆☆☆☆	☆☆☆☆☆	☆☆☆☆☆	☆☆☆☆☆

Review _____

_____

_____

_____

_____

_____

_____

_____

_____

_____

_____

_____

_____

Highlights and Quotes _____

_____

_____

_____

_____

_____

_____

_____

Questions _____

_____

_____

_____

_____

_____

Playlist _____

_____

_____

_____

_____

_____

Book Title and Author or Cover Art	Spice Level 🌶🌶🌶🌶🌶

Book Title and Author
or Cover Art

Spice Level 🌶🌶🌶🌶🌶

Format _____

Number of Pages _____

Date Started _____

Date Finished _____

Recommend _____

_____

_____

Characters	Plot	Writing	Overall
☆☆☆☆☆	☆☆☆☆☆☆	☆☆☆☆☆	☆☆☆☆☆

Review _____

_____

_____

_____

_____

_____

_____

_____

_____

_____

_____

_____

Highlights and Quotes _____

_____

_____

_____

_____

_____

_____

_____

Questions _____

_____

_____

_____

_____

_____

Playlist _____

_____

_____

_____

_____

_____

Book Title and Author or Cover Art	Spice Level 🌶🌶🌶🌶🌶

Format _____

Number of Pages _____

Date Started _____

Date Finished _____

Recommend _____

_____

_____

Characters	Plot	Writing	Overall
☆☆☆☆☆	☆☆☆☆☆☆	☆☆☆☆☆	☆☆☆☆☆

Review _____

_____

_____

_____

_____

_____

_____

_____

_____

_____

_____

_____

Highlights and Quotes _____

_____

_____

_____

_____

_____

_____

_____

Questions _____

_____

_____

_____

_____

_____

Playlist _____

_____

_____

_____

_____

_____

Book Title and Author or Cover Art	Spice Level 🌶🌶🌶🌶🌶
	Format _____
	Number of Pages _____
	Date Started _____
	Date Finished _____
	Recommend _____
	_____
	_____

Characters	Plot	Writing	Overall
☆☆☆☆☆	☆☆☆☆☆	☆☆☆☆☆	☆☆☆☆☆

Review _____

_____

_____

_____

_____

_____

_____

_____

_____

_____

_____

_____

_____

Highlights and Quotes _____

_____

_____

_____

_____

_____

_____

_____

Questions _____

_____

_____

_____

_____

_____

_____

Playlist _____

_____

_____

_____

_____

_____

Book Title and Author or Cover Art	Spice Level 🌶🌶🌶🌶🌶

Format _____

Number of Pages _____

Date Started _____

Date Finished _____

Recommend _____

_____

_____

Characters	Plot	Writing	Overall
☆☆☆☆☆	☆☆☆☆☆	☆☆☆☆☆	☆☆☆☆☆

Review _____

_____

_____

_____

_____

_____

_____

_____

_____

_____

_____

_____

_____

Highlights and Quotes _____

_____

_____

_____

_____

_____

_____

Questions _____

_____

_____

_____

_____

_____

Playlist _____

_____

_____

_____

_____

_____

| Book Title and Author or Cover Art | Spice Level 🌶🌶🌶🌶🌶 |

Book Title and Author
or Cover Art

Spice Level 🌶🌶🌶🌶🌶

Format _____

Number of Pages _____

Date Started _____

Date Finished _____

Recommend _____

_____

_____

| Characters | Plot | Writing | Overall |
| ☆☆☆☆☆ | ☆☆☆☆☆ | ☆☆☆☆☆ | ☆☆☆☆☆ |

Review _____

_____

_____

_____

_____

_____

_____

_____

_____

_____

_____

_____

Highlights and Quotes _____

_____

_____

_____

_____

_____

_____

_____

Questions _____

_____

_____

_____

_____

_____

Playlist _____

_____

_____

_____

_____

_____

Book Title and Author or Cover Art	Spice Level 🌶🌶🌶🌶🌶

Format _____

Number of Pages _____

Date Started _____

Date Finished _____

Recommend _____

_____

_____

Characters	Plot	Writing	Overall
☆☆☆☆☆	☆☆☆☆☆	☆☆☆☆☆	☆☆☆☆☆

Review _____

_____

_____

_____

_____

_____

_____

_____

_____

_____

_____

_____

_____

Highlights and Quotes _____

_____

_____

_____

_____

_____

_____

_____

Questions _____

_____

_____

_____

_____

_____

_____

Playlist _____

_____

_____

_____

_____

_____

_____

Book Title and Author or Cover Art	Spice Level 🌶🌶🌶🌶🌶

Format _____

Number of Pages _____

Date Started _____

Date Finished _____

Recommend _____

_____

_____

Characters	Plot	Writing	Overall
☆☆☆☆☆	☆☆☆☆☆	☆☆☆☆☆	☆☆☆☆☆

Review _____

_____

_____

_____

_____

_____

_____

_____

_____

_____

_____

_____

_____

Highlights and Quotes _____

_____

_____

_____

_____

_____

_____

_____

Questions _____

_____

_____

_____

_____

_____

Playlist _____

_____

_____

_____

_____

_____

Book Title and Author or Cover Art	Spice Level 🌶🌶🌶🌶🌶

Format _____

Number of Pages _____

Date Started _____

Date Finished _____

Recommend _____

_____

_____

Characters	Plot	Writing	Overall
☆☆☆☆☆	☆☆☆☆☆	☆☆☆☆☆	☆☆☆☆☆

Review _____

_____

_____

_____

_____

_____

_____

_____

_____

_____

_____

_____

Highlights and Quotes _____

_____

_____

_____

_____

_____

_____

_____

Questions _____

_____

_____

_____

_____

_____

_____

Playlist _____

_____

_____

_____

_____

_____

Book Title and Author or Cover Art	Spice Level 🌶🌶🌶🌶🌶

Format _____

Number of Pages _____

Date Started _____

Date Finished _____

Recommend _____

_____

_____

Characters	Plot	Writing	Overall
☆☆☆☆☆	☆☆☆☆☆	☆☆☆☆☆	☆☆☆☆☆

Review _____

_____

_____

_____

_____

_____

_____

_____

_____

_____

_____

_____

_____

Highlights and Quotes _____

_____

_____

_____

_____

_____

_____

_____

Questions _____

_____

_____

_____

_____

_____

_____

Playlist _____

_____

_____

_____

_____

_____

_____

| Book Title and Author or Cover Art | Spice Level 🌶🌶🌶🌶🌶 |

Book Title and Author
or Cover Art

Spice Level 🌶🌶🌶🌶🌶

Format _____

Number of Pages _____

Date Started _____

Date Finished _____

Recommend _____

_____

_____

Characters	Plot	Writing	Overall
☆☆☆☆☆	☆☆☆☆☆	☆☆☆☆☆	☆☆☆☆☆

Review _____

_____

_____

_____

_____

_____

_____

_____

_____

_____

_____

_____

Highlights and Quotes _____

_____

_____

_____

_____

_____

_____

_____

Questions _____

_____

_____

_____

_____

_____

Playlist _____

_____

_____

_____

_____

_____

Book Title and Author or Cover Art	Spice Level 🌶🌶🌶🌶🌶

Spice Level 🌶🌶🌶🌶🌶

Format _____

Number of Pages _____

Date Started _____

Date Finished _____

Recommend _____

_____

_____

Characters	Plot	Writing	Overall
☆☆☆☆☆	☆☆☆☆☆	☆☆☆☆☆	☆☆☆☆☆

Review _____

_____

_____

_____

_____

_____

_____

_____

_____

_____

_____

_____

Highlights and Quotes _____

_____

_____

_____

_____

_____

_____

Questions _____

_____

_____

_____

_____

_____

Playlist _____

_____

_____

_____

_____

_____

Book Title and Author or Cover Art	Spice Level 🌶🌶🌶🌶🌶
	Format _____
	Number of Pages _____
	Date Started _____
	Date Finished _____
	Recommend _____
	_____
	_____

Characters	Plot	Writing	Overall
☆☆☆☆☆	☆☆☆☆☆	☆☆☆☆☆	☆☆☆☆☆

Review _____

_____

_____

_____

_____

_____

_____

_____

_____

_____

_____

_____

_____

Highlights and Quotes _____

_____

_____

_____

_____

_____

_____

_____

Questions _____

_____

_____

_____

_____

_____

Playlist _____

_____

_____

_____

_____

_____

Book Title and Author or Cover Art	Spice Level 🌶🌶🌶🌶🌶
	Format _____
	Number of Pages _____
	Date Started _____
	Date Finished _____
	Recommend _____
	_____
	_____

Characters	Plot	Writing	Overall
☆☆☆☆☆	☆☆☆☆☆	☆☆☆☆☆	☆☆☆☆☆

Review _____

_____

_____

_____

_____

_____

_____

_____

_____

_____

_____

_____

_____

Highlights and Quotes _____

_____

_____

_____

_____

_____

_____

Questions _____

_____

_____

_____

_____

_____

Playlist _____

_____

_____

_____

_____

_____

Book Title and Author or Cover Art	Spice Level 🌶️🌶️🌶️🌶️🌶️

Format _____

Number of Pages _____

Date Started _____

Date Finished _____

Recommend _____

_____

_____

Characters	Plot	Writing	Overall
☆☆☆☆☆	☆☆☆☆☆	☆☆☆☆☆	☆☆☆☆☆

Review _____

_____

_____

_____

_____

_____

_____

_____

_____

_____

_____

_____

Highlights and Quotes _____

_____

_____

_____

_____

_____

_____

_____

Questions _____

_____

_____

_____

_____

_____

Playlist _____

_____

_____

_____

_____

_____

Book Title and Author or Cover Art	Spice Level 🌶🌶🌶🌶🌶
	Format _____
	Number of Pages _____
	Date Started _____
	Date Finished _____
	Recommend _____
	_____
	_____

Characters	Plot	Writing	Overall
☆☆☆☆☆	☆☆☆☆☆	☆☆☆☆☆	☆☆☆☆☆

Review _____

_____

_____

_____

_____

_____

_____

_____

_____

_____

_____

_____

Highlights and Quotes _____

_____

_____

_____

_____

_____

_____

_____

Questions _____

_____

_____

_____

_____

_____

_____

Playlist _____

_____

_____

_____

_____

_____

Book Title and Author or Cover Art	Spice Level 🌶🌶🌶🌶🌶

Format _____

Number of Pages _____

Date Started _____

Date Finished _____

Recommend _____

_____

_____

Characters	Plot	Writing	Overall
☆☆☆☆☆	☆☆☆☆☆	☆☆☆☆☆	☆☆☆☆☆

Review _____

_____

_____

_____

_____

_____

_____

_____

_____

_____

_____

_____

_____

_____

Highlights and Quotes _____

_____

_____

_____

_____

_____

_____

Questions _____

_____

_____

_____

_____

_____

Playlist _____

_____

_____

_____

_____

_____

Book Title and Author or Cover Art	Spice Level 🌶🌶🌶🌶
	Format _____
	Number of Pages _____
	Date Started _____
	Date Finished _____
	Recommend _____
	_____
	_____

Characters	Plot	Writing	Overall
☆☆☆☆☆	☆☆☆☆☆	☆☆☆☆☆	☆☆☆☆☆

Review _____

_____

_____

_____

_____

_____

_____

_____

_____

_____

_____

_____

_____

Highlights and Quotes _____

_____

_____

_____

_____

_____

_____

_____

Questions _____

_____

_____

_____

_____

_____

_____

Playlist _____

_____

_____

_____

_____

_____

_____

| Book Title and Author or Cover Art | Spice Level 🌶🌶🌶🌶🌶 |

Book Title and Author or Cover Art

Spice Level 🌶🌶🌶🌶🌶

Format _____

Number of Pages _____

Date Started _____

Date Finished _____

Recommend _____

_____

_____

Characters	Plot	Writing	Overall
☆☆☆☆☆	☆☆☆☆☆	☆☆☆☆☆	☆☆☆☆☆

Review _____

_____

_____

_____

_____

_____

_____

_____

_____

_____

_____

_____

_____

Highlights and Quotes _____

_____
_____
_____
_____
_____
_____
_____

Questions _____

_____
_____
_____
_____
_____

Playlist _____

_____
_____
_____
_____
_____

Book Title and Author or Cover Art	Spice Level 🌶🌶🌶🌶🌶
	Format _____
	Number of Pages _____
	Date Started _____
	Date Finished _____
	Recommend _____
	_____
	_____

Characters	Plot	Writing	Overall
☆☆☆☆☆	☆☆☆☆☆	☆☆☆☆☆	☆☆☆☆☆

Review _____

_____

_____

_____

_____

_____

_____

_____

_____

_____

_____

_____

_____

Highlights and Quotes _____

_____

_____

_____

_____

_____

_____

_____

Questions _____

_____

_____

_____

_____

_____

Playlist _____

_____

_____

_____

_____

_____

Book Title and Author or Cover Art	Spice Level 🌶🌶🌶🌶🌶

Format _____

Number of Pages _____

Date Started _____

Date Finished _____

Recommend _____

_____

_____

Characters	Plot	Writing	Overall
☆☆☆☆☆	☆☆☆☆☆	☆☆☆☆☆	☆☆☆☆☆

Review _____

_____

_____

_____

_____

_____

_____

_____

_____

_____

_____

_____

Highlights and Quotes _____

_____

_____

_____

_____

_____

_____

Questions _____

_____

_____

_____

_____

_____

Playlist _____

_____

_____

_____

_____

_____

Book Title and Author or Cover Art	Spice Level 🌶🌶🌶🌶🌶

Spice Level 🌶🌶🌶🌶🌶

Format _____

Number of Pages _____

Date Started _____

Date Finished _____

Recommend _____

_____

_____

Characters	Plot	Writing	Overall
☆☆☆☆☆	☆☆☆☆☆	☆☆☆☆☆	☆☆☆☆☆

Review _____

_____

_____

_____

_____

_____

_____

_____

_____

_____

_____

_____

_____

Highlights and Quotes _____

_____

_____

_____

_____

_____

_____

_____

Questions _____

_____

_____

_____

_____

_____

_____

Playlist _____

_____

_____

_____

_____

_____

Book Title and Author or Cover Art	Spice Level 🌶🌶🌶🌶🌶
	Format _____
	Number of Pages _____
	Date Started _____
	Date Finished _____
	Recommend _____
	_____
	_____

Characters	Plot	Writing	Overall
☆☆☆☆☆	☆☆☆☆☆	☆☆☆☆☆	☆☆☆☆☆

Review _____

_____

_____

_____

_____

_____

_____

_____

_____

_____

_____

_____

_____

Highlights and Quotes _____

_____

_____

_____

_____

_____

_____

_____

Questions _____

_____

_____

_____

_____

_____

Playlist _____

_____

_____

_____

_____

_____

| Book Title and Author or Cover Art | Spice Level 🌶🌶🌶🌶🌶 |

Spice Level 🌶🌶🌶🌶🌶

Format _____

Number of Pages _____

Date Started _____

Date Finished _____

Recommend _____

_____

_____

| Characters | Plot | Writing | Overall |
| ☆☆☆☆☆ | ☆☆☆☆☆ | ☆☆☆☆☆ | ☆☆☆☆☆ |

Review _____

_____

_____

_____

_____

_____

_____

_____

_____

_____

_____

_____

_____

Highlights and Quotes _____

_____

_____

_____

_____

_____

_____

_____

Questions _____

_____

_____

_____

_____

_____

_____

Playlist _____

_____

_____

_____

_____

_____

Book Title and Author or Cover Art	Spice Level 🌶🌶🌶🌶🌶
	Format _____
	Number of Pages _____
	Date Started _____
	Date Finished _____
	Recommend _____
	_____
	_____

Characters	Plot	Writing	Overall
☆☆☆☆☆	☆☆☆☆☆	☆☆☆☆☆	☆☆☆☆☆

Review _____

_____

_____

_____

_____

_____

_____

_____

_____

_____

_____

_____

_____

_____

Highlights and Quotes _____

_____

_____

_____

_____

_____

_____

_____

Questions _____

_____

_____

_____

_____

_____

_____

Playlist _____

_____

_____

_____

_____

_____

_____

Book Title and Author or Cover Art	Spice Level 🌶🌶🌶🌶🌶
	Format _____
	Number of Pages _____
	Date Started _____
	Date Finished _____
	Recommend _____
	_____
	_____

Characters	Plot	Writing	Overall
☆☆☆☆☆	☆☆☆☆☆	☆☆☆☆☆	☆☆☆☆☆

Review _____

_____

_____

_____

_____

_____

_____

_____

_____

_____

_____

_____

_____

Highlights and Quotes _____

_____

_____

_____

_____

_____

_____

Questions _____

_____

_____

_____

_____

_____

Playlist _____

_____

_____

_____

_____

_____

| Book Title and Author or Cover Art | Spice Level 🌶🌶🌶🌶🌶 |

Book Title and Author
or Cover Art

Spice Level 🌶🌶🌶🌶🌶

Format _____

Number of Pages _____

Date Started _____

Date Finished _____

Recommend _____

_____

_____

Characters	Plot	Writing	Overall
☆☆☆☆☆	☆☆☆☆☆	☆☆☆☆☆	☆☆☆☆☆

Review _____

_____

_____

_____

_____

_____

_____

_____

_____

_____

_____

_____

Highlights and Quotes _____

_____

_____

_____

_____

_____

_____

_____

Questions _____

_____

_____

_____

_____

_____

_____

Playlist _____

_____

_____

_____

_____

_____

_____

Book Title and Author or Cover Art	Spice Level 🌶🌶🌶🌶🌶
	Format _____
	Number of Pages _____
	Date Started _____
	Date Finished _____
	Recommend _____
	_____
	_____

Characters	Plot	Writing	Overall
☆☆☆☆☆	☆☆☆☆☆	☆☆☆☆☆	☆☆☆☆☆

Review _____

_____

_____

_____

_____

_____

_____

_____

_____

_____

_____

_____

_____

Highlights and Quotes _____

_____

_____

_____

_____

_____

_____

_____

Questions _____

_____

_____

_____

_____

_____

_____

Playlist _____

_____

_____

_____

_____

_____

_____

| Book Title and Author or Cover Art | Spice Level 🌶🌶🌶🌶🌶 |

Book Title and Author
or Cover Art

Spice Level 🌶🌶🌶🌶🌶

Format _____

Number of Pages _____

Date Started _____

Date Finished _____

Recommend _____

_____

_____

| Characters | Plot | Writing | Overall |
| ☆☆☆☆☆ | ☆☆☆☆☆ | ☆☆☆☆☆ | ☆☆☆☆☆ |

Review _____

_____

_____

_____

_____

_____

_____

_____

_____

_____

_____

_____

_____

Highlights and Quotes _____

_____

_____

_____

_____

_____

_____

_____

Questions _____

_____

_____

_____

_____

_____

_____

Playlist _____

_____

_____

_____

_____

_____

| Book Title and Author or Cover Art | Spice Level 🌶🌶🌶🌶🌶 |

Book Title and Author or Cover Art

Spice Level 🌶🌶🌶🌶🌶

Format _____

Number of Pages _____

Date Started _____

Date Finished _____

Recommend _____

_____

_____

Characters	Plot	Writing	Overall
☆☆☆☆☆	☆☆☆☆☆	☆☆☆☆☆	☆☆☆☆☆

Review _____

_____

_____

_____

_____

_____

_____

_____

_____

_____

_____

_____

Highlights and Quotes _____

_____

_____

_____

_____

_____

_____

Questions _____

_____

_____

_____

_____

_____

Playlist _____

_____

_____

_____

_____

_____

Book Title and Author or Cover Art	Spice Level 🌶🌶🌶🌶🌶
	Format _____
	Number of Pages _____
	Date Started _____
	Date Finished _____
	Recommend _____
	_____
	_____

Characters	Plot	Writing	Overall
☆☆☆☆☆	☆☆☆☆☆	☆☆☆☆☆	☆☆☆☆☆

Review _____

_____

_____

_____

_____

_____

_____

_____

_____

_____

_____

_____

_____

Highlights and Quotes _____

_____

_____

_____

_____

_____

_____

Questions _____

_____

_____

_____

_____

_____

_____

Playlist _____

_____

_____

_____

_____

_____

| Book Title and Author or Cover Art | Spice Level 🌶🌶🌶🌶🌶 |

Spice Level 🌶🌶🌶🌶🌶

Format _____

Number of Pages _____

Date Started _____

Date Finished _____

Recommend _____

_____

_____

Characters	Plot	Writing	Overall
☆☆☆☆☆	☆☆☆☆☆	☆☆☆☆☆	☆☆☆☆☆

Review _____

_____

_____

_____

_____

_____

_____

_____

_____

_____

_____

_____

_____

Highlights and Quotes _____

_____

_____

_____

_____

_____

_____

Questions _____

_____

_____

_____

_____

_____

Playlist _____

_____

_____

_____

_____

_____

Book Title and Author or Cover Art	Spice Level 🌶🌶🌶🌶🌶

Format _____

Number of Pages _____

Date Started _____

Date Finished _____

Recommend _____

_____

_____

Characters	Plot	Writing	Overall
☆☆☆☆☆	☆☆☆☆☆	☆☆☆☆☆	☆☆☆☆☆

Review _____

_____

_____

_____

_____

_____

_____

_____

_____

_____

_____

_____

_____

Highlights and Quotes _____

_____

_____

_____

_____

_____

_____

_____

Questions _____

_____

_____

_____

_____

_____

_____

Playlist _____

_____

_____

_____

_____

_____

_____

Book Title and Author or Cover Art	Spice Level 🌶🌶🌶🌶🌶
	Format _____
	Number of Pages _____
	Date Started _____
	Date Finished _____
	Recommend _____
	_____
	_____

Characters	Plot	Writing	Overall
☆☆☆☆☆	☆☆☆☆☆	☆☆☆☆☆	☆☆☆☆☆

Review _____

_____

_____

_____

_____

_____

_____

_____

_____

_____

_____

_____

_____

Highlights and Quotes _____

_____

_____

_____

_____

_____

_____

_____

Questions _____

_____

_____

_____

_____

_____

Playlist _____

_____

_____

_____

_____

_____

Book Title and Author or Cover Art	Spice Level 🌶🌶🌶🌶🌶

Format _____

Number of Pages _____

Date Started _____

Date Finished _____

Recommend _____

_____

_____

Characters	Plot	Writing	Overall
☆☆☆☆☆	☆☆☆☆☆	☆☆☆☆☆	☆☆☆☆☆

Review _____

_____

_____

_____

_____

_____

_____

_____

_____

_____

_____

_____

_____

Highlights and Quotes _____

_____

_____

_____

_____

_____

_____

_____

Questions _____

_____

_____

_____

_____

_____

_____

Playlist _____

_____

_____

_____

_____

_____

_____

Book Title and Author or Cover Art	Spice Level 🌶🌶🌶🌶🌶

Format _____

Number of Pages _____

Date Started _____

Date Finished _____

Recommend _____

_____

_____

Characters	Plot	Writing	Overall
☆☆☆☆☆	☆☆☆☆☆	☆☆☆☆☆	☆☆☆☆☆

Review _____

_____

_____

_____

_____

_____

_____

_____

_____

_____

_____

_____

Highlights and Quotes _____

_____

_____

_____

_____

_____

_____

_____

Questions _____

_____

_____

_____

_____

_____

Playlist _____

_____

_____

_____

_____

_____

Book Title and Author or Cover Art	Spice Level 🌶🌶🌶🌶🌶

Format _____

Number of Pages _____

Date Started _____

Date Finished _____

Recommend _____

_____

_____

Characters	Plot	Writing	Overall
☆☆☆☆☆	☆☆☆☆☆	☆☆☆☆☆	☆☆☆☆☆

Review _____

_____

_____

_____

_____

_____

_____

_____

_____

_____

_____

_____

_____

Highlights and Quotes _____

_____

_____

_____

_____

_____

_____

_____

Questions _____

_____

_____

_____

_____

_____

_____

Playlist _____

_____

_____

_____

_____

_____

Book Title and Author or Cover Art	Spice Level 🌶🌶🌶🌶🌶
	Format _____
	Number of Pages _____
	Date Started _____
	Date Finished _____
	Recommend _____
	_____
	_____

Characters	Plot	Writing	Overall
☆☆☆☆☆	☆☆☆☆☆	☆☆☆☆☆	☆☆☆☆☆

Review _____

_____

_____

_____

_____

_____

_____

_____

_____

_____

_____

_____

_____

Highlights and Quotes _____

_____

_____

_____

_____

_____

_____

_____

Questions _____

_____

_____

_____

_____

_____

Playlist _____

_____

_____

_____

_____

_____

Book Title and Author or Cover Art	Spice Level 🌶️🌶️🌶️🌶️🌶️

Format _____

Number of Pages _____

Date Started _____

Date Finished _____

Recommend _____

_____

_____

Characters	Plot	Writing	Overall
☆☆☆☆☆	☆☆☆☆☆	☆☆☆☆☆	☆☆☆☆☆

Review _____

_____

_____

_____

_____

_____

_____

_____

_____

_____

_____

_____

Highlights and Quotes _____

_____

_____

_____

_____

_____

_____

Questions _____

_____

_____

_____

_____

_____

Playlist _____

_____

_____

_____

_____

_____

Book Title and Author or Cover Art	Spice Level 🌶🌶🌶🌶🌶
	Format _____
	Number of Pages _____
	Date Started _____
	Date Finished _____
	Recommend _____
	_____
	_____

Characters	Plot	Writing	Overall
☆☆☆☆☆	☆☆☆☆☆	☆☆☆☆☆	☆☆☆☆☆

Review _____

_____

_____

_____

_____

_____

_____

_____

_____

_____

_____

_____

_____

Highlights and Quotes _____

_____

_____

_____

_____

_____

_____

_____

Questions _____

_____

_____

_____

_____

_____

_____

Playlist _____

_____

_____

_____

_____

_____

Book Title and Author or Cover Art	Spice Level 🌶🌶🌶🌶🌶

Book Title and Author
or Cover Art

Spice Level 🌶🌶🌶🌶🌶

Format _____

Number of Pages _____

Date Started _____

Date Finished _____

Recommend _____

_____

_____

Characters	Plot	Writing	Overall
☆☆☆☆☆	☆☆☆☆☆	☆☆☆☆☆	☆☆☆☆☆

Review _____

_____

_____

_____

_____

_____

_____

_____

_____

_____

_____

_____

Highlights and Quotes _____

_____

_____

_____

_____

_____

_____

_____

Questions _____

_____

_____

_____

_____

_____

Playlist _____

_____

_____

_____

_____

_____

Book Title and Author or Cover Art	Spice Level 🌶🌶🌶🌶🌶

Format _____

Number of Pages _____

Date Started _____

Date Finished _____

Recommend _____

_____

_____

Characters	Plot	Writing	Overall
☆☆☆☆☆	☆☆☆☆☆	☆☆☆☆☆	☆☆☆☆☆

Review _____

_____

_____

_____

_____

_____

_____

_____

_____

_____

_____

_____

Highlights and Quotes _____

_____

_____

_____

_____

_____

_____

Questions _____

_____

_____

_____

_____

_____

Playlist _____

_____

_____

_____

_____

_____

Book Title and Author or Cover Art	Spice Level 🌶🌶🌶🌶🌶
	Format _____
	Number of Pages _____
	Date Started _____
	Date Finished _____
	Recommend _____
	_____
	_____

Characters	Plot	Writing	Overall
☆☆☆☆☆	☆☆☆☆☆	☆☆☆☆☆	☆☆☆☆☆

Review _____

_____

_____

_____

_____

_____

_____

_____

_____

_____

_____

_____

_____

Highlights and Quotes _____

_____

_____

_____

_____

_____

_____

_____

Questions _____

_____

_____

_____

_____

_____

_____

Playlist _____

_____

_____

_____

_____

_____

Book Title and Author or Cover Art	Spice Level 🌶🌶🌶🌶🌶
	Format _____
	Number of Pages _____
	Date Started _____
	Date Finished _____
	Recommend _____
	_____
	_____

Characters	Plot	Writing	Overall
☆☆☆☆☆	☆☆☆☆☆	☆☆☆☆☆	☆☆☆☆☆

Review _____

_____

_____

_____

_____

_____

_____

_____

_____

_____

_____

_____

_____

Highlights and Quotes _____

_____

_____

_____

_____

_____

_____

Questions _____

_____

_____

_____

_____

_____

Playlist _____

_____

_____

_____

_____

_____

| Book Title and Author or Cover Art | Spice Level 🌶🌶🌶🌶🌶 |

Book Title and Author
or Cover Art

Spice Level 🌶🌶🌶🌶🌶

Format _____

Number of Pages _____

Date Started _____

Date Finished _____

Recommend _____

_____

_____

| Characters | Plot | Writing | Overall |
| ☆☆☆☆☆ | ☆☆☆☆☆ | ☆☆☆☆☆ | ☆☆☆☆☆ |

Review _____

_____

_____

_____

_____

_____

_____

_____

_____

_____

_____

_____

Highlights and Quotes _____

_____

_____

_____

_____

_____

_____

_____

Questions _____

_____

_____

_____

_____

_____

Playlist _____

_____

_____

_____

_____

_____

Book Title and Author or Cover Art	Spice Level 🌶️🌶️🌶️🌶️🌶️

Format _____

Number of Pages _____

Date Started _____

Date Finished _____

Recommend _____

_____

_____

Characters	Plot	Writing	Overall
☆☆☆☆☆	☆☆☆☆☆	☆☆☆☆☆	☆☆☆☆☆

Review _____

_____

_____

_____

_____

_____

_____

_____

_____

_____

_____

_____

_____

Highlights and Quotes _____

_____

_____

_____

_____

_____

_____

_____

Questions _____

_____

_____

_____

_____

_____

Playlist _____

_____

_____

_____

_____

_____

| Book Title and Author or Cover Art | Spice Level 🌶🌶🌶🌶🌶 |

Book Title and Author or Cover Art

Spice Level 🌶🌶🌶🌶🌶

Format _____

Number of Pages _____

Date Started _____

Date Finished _____

Recommend _____

_____

_____

Characters	Plot	Writing	Overall
☆☆☆☆☆	☆☆☆☆☆	☆☆☆☆☆	☆☆☆☆☆

Review _____

_____

_____

_____

_____

_____

_____

_____

_____

_____

_____

_____

_____

_____

Highlights and Quotes _____

_____

_____

_____

_____

_____

_____

Questions _____

_____

_____

_____

_____

_____

_____

Playlist _____

_____

_____

_____

_____

_____

Book Title and Author or Cover Art	Spice Level 🌶🌶🌶🌶🌶
	Format _____
	Number of Pages _____
	Date Started _____
	Date Finished _____
	Recommend _____
	_____
	_____

Characters	Plot	Writing	Overall
☆☆☆☆☆	☆☆☆☆☆	☆☆☆☆☆	☆☆☆☆☆

Review _____

_____

_____

_____

_____

_____

_____

_____

_____

_____

_____

_____

Highlights and Quotes _____

_____

_____

_____

_____

_____

_____

_____

Questions _____

_____

_____

_____

_____

_____

Playlist _____

_____

_____

_____

_____

_____

Book Title and Author or Cover Art	Spice Level 🌶🌶🌶🌶🌶
	Format _____
	Number of Pages _____
	Date Started _____
	Date Finished _____
	Recommend _____
	_____
	_____

Characters	Plot	Writing	Overall
☆☆☆☆☆	☆☆☆☆☆	☆☆☆☆☆	☆☆☆☆☆

Review _____

_____

_____

_____

_____

_____

_____

_____

_____

_____

_____

_____

_____

Highlights and Quotes _____

_____

_____

_____

_____

_____

_____

_____

Questions _____

_____

_____

_____

_____

_____

_____

Playlist _____

_____

_____

_____

_____

_____

_____

Book Title and Author or Cover Art	Spice Level 🌶🌶🌶🌶🌶

Format _____

Number of Pages _____

Date Started _____

Date Finished _____

Recommend _____

_____

_____

Characters	Plot	Writing	Overall
☆☆☆☆☆	☆☆☆☆☆	☆☆☆☆☆	☆☆☆☆☆

Review _____

_____

_____

_____

_____

_____

_____

_____

_____

_____

_____

_____

_____

Highlights and Quotes _____

_____

_____

_____

_____

_____

_____

Questions _____

_____

_____

_____

_____

_____

Playlist _____

_____

_____

_____

_____

_____

Book Title and Author or Cover Art	Spice Level 🌶🌶🌶🌶🌶

Format _____

Number of Pages _____

Date Started _____

Date Finished _____

Recommend _____

_____

_____

Characters	Plot	Writing	Overall
☆☆☆☆☆	☆☆☆☆☆	☆☆☆☆☆	☆☆☆☆☆

Review _____

_____

_____

_____

_____

_____

_____

_____

_____

_____

_____

_____

Highlights and Quotes _____

_____

_____

_____

_____

_____

_____

_____

Questions _____

_____

_____

_____

_____

_____

Playlist _____

_____

_____

_____

_____

_____

Book Title and Author or Cover Art	Spice Level 🌶🌶🌶🌶🌶
	Format _____
	Number of Pages _____
	Date Started _____
	Date Finished _____
	Recommend _____
	_____
	_____

Characters	Plot	Writing	Overall
☆☆☆☆☆	☆☆☆☆☆	☆☆☆☆☆	☆☆☆☆☆

Review _____

_____

_____

_____

_____

_____

_____

_____

_____

_____

_____

_____

_____

Highlights and Quotes _____

_____

_____

_____

_____

_____

_____

_____

Questions _____

_____

_____

_____

_____

_____

Playlist _____

_____

_____

_____

_____

_____

Book Title and Author or Cover Art	Spice Level 🌶🌶🌶🌶🌶

Book Title and Author or Cover Art

Spice Level 🌶🌶🌶🌶🌶

Format _____

Number of Pages _____

Date Started _____

Date Finished _____

Recommend _____

_____

_____

Characters	Plot	Writing	Overall
☆☆☆☆☆	☆☆☆☆☆	☆☆☆☆☆	☆☆☆☆☆

Review _____

_____

_____

_____

_____

_____

_____

_____

_____

_____

_____

_____

_____

Highlights and Quotes _____

_____

_____

_____

_____

_____

_____

Questions _____

_____

_____

_____

_____

_____

Playlist _____

_____

_____

_____

_____

_____

Book Title and Author or Cover Art	Spice Level 🌶🌶🌶🌶🌶
	Format _____
	Number of Pages _____
	Date Started _____
	Date Finished _____
	Recommend _____
	_____
	_____

Characters	Plot	Writing	Overall
☆☆☆☆☆	☆☆☆☆☆	☆☆☆☆☆	☆☆☆☆☆

Review _____

_____

_____

_____

_____

_____

_____

_____

_____

_____

_____

_____

Highlights and Quotes _____

_____

_____

_____

_____

_____

_____

Questions _____

_____

_____

_____

_____

_____

Playlist _____

_____

_____

_____

_____

_____

Book Title and Author or Cover Art	Spice Level 🌶🌶🌶🌶🌶
	Format _____
	Number of Pages _____
	Date Started _____
	Date Finished _____
	Recommend _____
	_____
	_____

Characters	Plot	Writing	Overall
☆☆☆☆☆	☆☆☆☆☆	☆☆☆☆☆	☆☆☆☆☆

Review _____

_____

_____

_____

_____

_____

_____

_____

_____

_____

_____

_____

_____

_____

Highlights and Quotes _____

_____

_____

_____

_____

_____

_____

_____

Questions _____

_____

_____

_____

_____

_____

Playlist _____

_____

_____

_____

_____

_____

| Book Title and Author or Cover Art | Spice Level 🌶🌶🌶🌶🌶 |

Spice Level 🌶🌶🌶🌶🌶

Format _____

Number of Pages _____

Date Started _____

Date Finished _____

Recommend _____

_____

_____

| Characters | Plot | Writing | Overall |
| ☆☆☆☆☆ | ☆☆☆☆☆ | ☆☆☆☆☆ | ☆☆☆☆☆ |

Review _____

_____

_____

_____

_____

_____

_____

_____

_____

_____

_____

_____

Highlights and Quotes _____

_____

_____

_____

_____

_____

_____

Questions _____

_____

_____

_____

_____

_____

Playlist _____

_____

_____

_____

_____

_____

Book Title and Author or Cover Art	Spice Level 🌶🌶🌶🌶🌶

Format _____

Number of Pages _____

Date Started _____

Date Finished _____

Recommend _____

_____

_____

Characters	Plot	Writing	Overall
☆☆☆☆☆	☆☆☆☆☆	☆☆☆☆☆	☆☆☆☆☆

Review _____

_____

_____

_____

_____

_____

_____

_____

_____

_____

_____

_____

Highlights and Quotes _____

_____

_____

_____

_____

_____

_____

Questions _____

_____

_____

_____

_____

_____

Playlist _____

_____

_____

_____

_____

_____

Book Title and Author or Cover Art	Spice Level 🌶🌶🌶🌶🌶
	Format _____
	Number of Pages _____
	Date Started _____
	Date Finished _____
	Recommend _____
	_____
	_____

Characters	Plot	Writing	Overall
☆☆☆☆☆	☆☆☆☆☆	☆☆☆☆☆	☆☆☆☆☆

Review _____

_____

_____

_____

_____

_____

_____

_____

_____

_____

_____

_____

_____

Highlights and Quotes _____

_____

_____

_____

_____

_____

_____

_____

Questions _____

_____

_____

_____

_____

_____

Playlist _____

_____

_____

_____

_____

_____

Book Title and Author or Cover Art	Spice Level 🌶🌶🌶🌶🌶

Format _____

Number of Pages _____

Date Started _____

Date Finished _____

Recommend _____

_____

_____

Characters	Plot	Writing	Overall
☆☆☆☆☆	☆☆☆☆☆☆	☆☆☆☆☆	☆☆☆☆☆

Review _____

_____

_____

_____

_____

_____

_____

_____

_____

_____

_____

_____

Highlights and Quotes _____

_____

_____

_____

_____

_____

_____

Questions _____

_____

_____

_____

_____

_____

Playlist _____

_____

_____

_____

_____

_____

_____

Book Title and Author or Cover Art	Spice Level 🌶🌶🌶🌶🌶
	Format _____
	Number of Pages _____
	Date Started _____
	Date Finished _____
	Recommend _____
	_____
	_____

Characters	Plot	Writing	Overall
☆☆☆☆☆	☆☆☆☆☆☆	☆☆☆☆☆☆	☆☆☆☆☆

Review _____

_____

_____

_____

_____

_____

_____

_____

_____

_____

_____

_____

Highlights and Quotes _____

_____

_____

_____

_____

_____

_____

_____

Questions _____

_____

_____

_____

_____

_____

_____

Playlist _____

_____

_____

_____

_____

_____

Book Title and Author or Cover Art	Spice Level 🌶🌶🌶🌶🌶
	Format _____
	Number of Pages _____
	Date Started _____
	Date Finished _____
	Recommend _____
	_____
	_____

Characters	Plot	Writing	Overall
☆☆☆☆☆	☆☆☆☆☆	☆☆☆☆☆	☆☆☆☆☆

Review _____

_____

_____

_____

_____

_____

_____

_____

_____

_____

_____

_____

_____

_____

Highlights and Quotes _____

_____

_____

_____

_____

_____

_____

_____

Questions _____

_____

_____

_____

_____

_____

Playlist _____

_____

_____

_____

_____

_____

| Book Title and Author or Cover Art | Spice Level 🌶🌶🌶🌶🌶 |

Spice Level 🌶🌶🌶🌶🌶

Format _____

Number of Pages _____

Date Started _____

Date Finished _____

Recommend _____

_____

_____

Characters	Plot	Writing	Overall
☆☆☆☆☆	☆☆☆☆☆	☆☆☆☆☆	☆☆☆☆☆

Review _____

_____

_____

_____

_____

_____

_____

_____

_____

_____

_____

_____

Highlights and Quotes _____

_____

_____

_____

_____

_____

_____

Questions _____

_____

_____

_____

_____

_____

Playlist _____

_____

_____

_____

_____

_____

Book Title and Author or Cover Art	Spice Level 🌶🌶🌶🌶🌶

Format _____

Number of Pages _____

Date Started _____

Date Finished _____

Recommend _____

_____

_____

Characters	Plot	Writing	Overall
☆☆☆☆☆	☆☆☆☆☆	☆☆☆☆☆	☆☆☆☆☆

Review _____

_____

_____

_____

_____

_____

_____

_____

_____

_____

_____

_____

_____

Highlights and Quotes _____

_____

_____

_____

_____

_____

_____

_____

Questions _____

_____

_____

_____

_____

_____

Playlist _____

_____

_____

_____

_____

_____

Book Title and Author or Cover Art	Spice Level 🌶🌶🌶🌶🌶

Format _____

Number of Pages _____

Date Started _____

Date Finished _____

Recommend _____

_____

_____

Characters	Plot	Writing	Overall
☆☆☆☆☆	☆☆☆☆☆	☆☆☆☆☆	☆☆☆☆☆

Review _____

_____

_____

_____

_____

_____

_____

_____

_____

_____

_____

_____

_____

Highlights and Quotes _____

_____

_____

_____

_____

_____

_____

Questions _____

_____

_____

_____

_____

_____

Playlist _____

_____

_____

_____

_____

_____

Book Title and Author or Cover Art	Spice Level 🌶🌶🌶🌶🌶
	Format _____
	Number of Pages _____
	Date Started _____
	Date Finished _____
	Recommend _____
	_____
	_____

Characters	Plot	Writing	Overall
☆☆☆☆☆	☆☆☆☆☆	☆☆☆☆☆	☆☆☆☆☆

Review _____

_____

_____

_____

_____

_____

_____

_____

_____

_____

_____

_____

Highlights and Quotes _____

_____

_____

_____

_____

_____

_____

Questions _____

_____

_____

_____

_____

_____

Playlist _____

_____

_____

_____

_____

_____

Book Title and Author or Cover Art	Spice Level 🌶🌶🌶🌶🌶

Format _____

Number of Pages _____

Date Started _____

Date Finished _____

Recommend _____

_____

_____

Characters	Plot	Writing	Overall
☆☆☆☆☆	☆☆☆☆☆	☆☆☆☆☆	☆☆☆☆☆

Review _____

_____

_____

_____

_____

_____

_____

_____

_____

_____

_____

_____

_____

Highlights and Quotes _____

_____
_____
_____
_____
_____
_____

Questions _____

_____
_____
_____
_____
_____

Playlist _____

_____
_____
_____
_____
_____

Book Title and Author or Cover Art	Spice Level 🌶🌶🌶🌶🌶
	Format _____
	Number of Pages _____
	Date Started _____
	Date Finished _____
	Recommend _____
	_____
	_____

Characters	Plot	Writing	Overall
☆☆☆☆☆	☆☆☆☆☆	☆☆☆☆☆	☆☆☆☆☆

Review _____

_____

_____

_____

_____

_____

_____

_____

_____

_____

_____

_____

_____

Highlights and Quotes _____

_____

_____

_____

_____

_____

_____

Questions _____

_____

_____

_____

_____

_____

Playlist _____

_____

_____

_____

_____

_____

| Book Title and Author or Cover Art | Spice Level 🌶🌶🌶🌶🌶 |

Book Title and Author or Cover Art

Spice Level 🌶🌶🌶🌶🌶

Format _____

Number of Pages _____

Date Started _____

Date Finished _____

Recommend _____

_____

_____

| Characters | Plot | Writing | Overall |
| ☆☆☆☆☆ | ☆☆☆☆☆ | ☆☆☆☆☆ | ☆☆☆☆☆ |

Review _____

_____

_____

_____

_____

_____

_____

_____

_____

_____

_____

_____

_____

Highlights and Quotes _____

_____
_____
_____
_____
_____
_____

Questions _____

_____
_____
_____
_____
_____

Playlist _____

_____
_____
_____
_____
_____

Book Title and Author or Cover Art	Spice Level 🌶🌶🌶🌶🌶

Format _____

Number of Pages _____

Date Started _____

Date Finished _____

Recommend _____

_____

_____

Characters	Plot	Writing	Overall
☆☆☆☆☆	☆☆☆☆☆☆	☆☆☆☆☆☆	☆☆☆☆☆

Review _____

_____

_____

_____

_____

_____

_____

_____

_____

_____

_____

_____

Highlights and Quotes _____

_____

_____

_____

_____

_____

_____

_____

Questions _____

_____

_____

_____

_____

_____

Playlist _____

_____

_____

_____

_____

_____

Book Title and Author or Cover Art	Spice Level 🌶️🌶️🌶️🌶️🌶️
	Format _____
	Number of Pages _____
	Date Started _____
	Date Finished _____
	Recommend _____
	_____
	_____

Characters	Plot	Writing	Overall
☆☆☆☆☆	☆☆☆☆☆	☆☆☆☆☆	☆☆☆☆☆

Review _____

_____

_____

_____

_____

_____

_____

_____

_____

_____

_____

_____

_____

Highlights and Quotes _____

_____

_____

_____

_____

_____

_____

_____

Questions _____

_____

_____

_____

_____

_____

Playlist _____

_____

_____

_____

_____

_____

_____

Book Title and Author or Cover Art	Spice Level 🌶🌶🌶🌶🌶

Format _____

Number of Pages _____

Date Started _____

Date Finished _____

Recommend _____

_____

_____

Characters	Plot	Writing	Overall
☆☆☆☆☆	☆☆☆☆☆	☆☆☆☆☆	☆☆☆☆☆

Review _____

_____

_____

_____

_____

_____

_____

_____

_____

_____

_____

_____

Highlights and Quotes _____

_____

_____

_____

_____

_____

_____

_____

Questions _____

_____

_____

_____

_____

_____

Playlist _____

_____

_____

_____

_____

_____

Book Title and Author or Cover Art	Spice Level 🌶🌶🌶🌶🌶

Spice Level 🌶🌶🌶🌶🌶

Format _____

Number of Pages _____

Date Started _____

Date Finished _____

Recommend _____

_____

_____

Characters	Plot	Writing	Overall
☆☆☆☆☆	☆☆☆☆☆	☆☆☆☆☆	☆☆☆☆☆

Review _____

_____

_____

_____

_____

_____

_____

_____

_____

_____

_____

_____

Highlights and Quotes _____

_____

_____

_____

_____

_____

_____

Questions _____

_____

_____

_____

_____

_____

Playlist _____

_____

_____

_____

_____

_____

Book Title and Author or Cover Art	Spice Level 🌶🌶🌶🌶🌶
	Format _____
	Number of Pages _____
	Date Started _____
	Date Finished _____
	Recommend _____
	_____
	_____

Characters	Plot	Writing	Overall
☆☆☆☆☆	☆☆☆☆☆	☆☆☆☆☆	☆☆☆☆☆

Review _____

_____

_____

_____

_____

_____

_____

_____

_____

_____

_____

_____

Highlights and Quotes _____

_____

_____

_____

_____

_____

_____

_____

Questions _____

_____

_____

_____

_____

_____

_____

Playlist _____

_____

_____

_____

_____

_____

_____

Book Title and Author or Cover Art	Spice Level ♨♨♨♨♨
	Format _____
	Number of Pages _____
	Date Started _____
	Date Finished _____
	Recommend _____
	_____
	_____

Characters	Plot	Writing	Overall
☆☆☆☆☆	☆☆☆☆☆	☆☆☆☆☆	☆☆☆☆☆

Review _____

_____

_____

_____

_____

_____

_____

_____

_____

_____

_____

_____

_____

Highlights and Quotes _____

_____

_____

_____

_____

_____

_____

Questions _____

_____

_____

_____

_____

_____

Playlist _____

_____

_____

_____

_____

_____

Book Title and Author or Cover Art	Spice Level 🌶🌶🌶🌶🌶
	Format _____
	Number of Pages _____
	Date Started _____
	Date Finished _____
	Recommend _____
	_____
	_____

Characters	Plot	Writing	Overall
☆☆☆☆☆	☆☆☆☆☆	☆☆☆☆☆	☆☆☆☆☆

Review _____

_____

_____

_____

_____

_____

_____

_____

_____

_____

_____

_____

_____

_____

Highlights and Quotes _____

_____

_____

_____

_____

_____

_____

Questions _____

_____

_____

_____

_____

_____

Playlist _____

_____

_____

_____

_____

_____

Book Title and Author or Cover Art	Spice Level 🌶🌶🌶🌶🌶
	Format _____
	Number of Pages _____
	Date Started _____
	Date Finished _____
	Recommend _____
	_____
	_____

Characters	Plot	Writing	Overall
☆☆☆☆☆	☆☆☆☆☆	☆☆☆☆☆	☆☆☆☆☆

Review _____

_____

_____

_____

_____

_____

_____

_____

_____

_____

_____

_____

_____

Highlights and Quotes _____

_____

_____

_____

_____

_____

_____

_____

Questions _____

_____

_____

_____

_____

_____

_____

Playlist _____

_____

_____

_____

_____

_____

Book Title and Author or Cover Art	Spice Level 🌶🌶🌶🌶🌶

Format _____

Number of Pages _____

Date Started _____

Date Finished _____

Recommend _____

_____

_____

Characters	Plot	Writing	Overall
☆☆☆☆☆	☆☆☆☆☆	☆☆☆☆☆	☆☆☆☆☆

Review _____

_____

_____

_____

_____

_____

_____

_____

_____

_____

_____

_____

Highlights and Quotes _____

_____

_____

_____

_____

_____

_____

Questions _____

_____

_____

_____

_____

_____

Playlist _____

_____

_____

_____

_____

_____

Book Title and Author or Cover Art	Spice Level 🌶🌶🌶🌶🌶
	Format _____
	Number of Pages _____
	Date Started _____
	Date Finished _____
	Recommend _____
	_____
	_____

Characters	Plot	Writing	Overall
☆☆☆☆☆	☆☆☆☆☆	☆☆☆☆☆	☆☆☆☆☆

Review _____

_____

_____

_____

_____

_____

_____

_____

_____

_____

_____

_____

Highlights and Quotes _____

_____

_____

_____

_____

_____

_____

_____

Questions _____

_____

_____

_____

_____

_____

Playlist _____

_____

_____

_____

_____

_____

| Book Title and Author or Cover Art | Spice Level 🌶🌶🌶🌶🌶 |

Book Title and Author
or Cover Art

Spice Level 🌶🌶🌶🌶🌶

Format _____

Number of Pages _____

Date Started _____

Date Finished _____

Recommend _____

_____

_____

| Characters | Plot | Writing | Overall |
| ☆☆☆☆☆ | ☆☆☆☆☆ | ☆☆☆☆☆ | ☆☆☆☆☆ |

Review _____

_____

_____

_____

_____

_____

_____

_____

_____

_____

_____

_____

Highlights and Quotes _____

_____

_____

_____

_____

_____

_____

_____

Questions _____

_____

_____

_____

_____

_____

Playlist _____

_____

_____

_____

_____

_____

Book Title and Author or Cover Art	Spice Level 🌶🌶🌶🌶🌶

Format _____

Number of Pages _____

Date Started _____

Date Finished _____

Recommend _____

_____

_____

Characters	Plot	Writing	Overall
☆☆☆☆☆	☆☆☆☆☆	☆☆☆☆☆	☆☆☆☆☆

Review _____

_____

_____

_____

_____

_____

_____

_____

_____

_____

_____

_____

_____

_____

Highlights and Quotes _____

_____

_____

_____

_____

_____

_____

Questions _____

_____

_____

_____

_____

_____

Playlist _____

_____

_____

_____

_____

_____

| Book Title and Author or Cover Art | Spice Level 🌶🌶🌶🌶🌶 |

Spice Level 🌶🌶🌶🌶🌶

Format _____

Number of Pages _____

Date Started _____

Date Finished _____

Recommend _____

_____

_____

Characters	Plot	Writing	Overall
☆☆☆☆☆	☆☆☆☆☆	☆☆☆☆☆	☆☆☆☆☆

Review _____

_____

_____

_____

_____

_____

_____

_____

_____

_____

_____

_____

_____

Highlights and Quotes _____

_____

_____

_____

_____

_____

_____

_____

Questions _____

_____

_____

_____

_____

_____

Playlist _____

_____

_____

_____

_____

_____

Book Title and Author or Cover Art	Spice Level 🌶🌶🌶🌶🌶

Format _____

Number of Pages _____

Date Started _____

Date Finished _____

Recommend _____

_____

_____

Characters	Plot	Writing	Overall
☆☆☆☆☆	☆☆☆☆☆	☆☆☆☆☆	☆☆☆☆☆

Review _____

_____

_____

_____

_____

_____

_____

_____

_____

_____

_____

_____

_____

Highlights and Quotes _____

_____

_____

_____

_____

_____

_____

Questions _____

_____

_____

_____

_____

_____

Playlist _____

_____

_____

_____

_____

_____

| Book Title and Author or Cover Art | Spice Level 🌶🌶🌶🌶🌶 |

Book Title and Author
or Cover Art

Spice Level 🌶🌶🌶🌶🌶

Format _____

Number of Pages _____

Date Started _____

Date Finished _____

Recommend _____

_____

_____

Characters	Plot	Writing	Overall
☆☆☆☆☆	☆☆☆☆☆	☆☆☆☆☆	☆☆☆☆☆

Review _____

_____

_____

_____

_____

_____

_____

_____

_____

_____

_____

_____

_____

Highlights and Quotes _____

_____

_____

_____

_____

_____

_____

Questions _____

_____

_____

_____

_____

_____

Playlist _____

_____

_____

_____

_____

_____

Book Title and Author or Cover Art	Spice Level 🌶🌶🌶🌶🌶

Format _____

Number of Pages _____

Date Started _____

Date Finished _____

Recommend _____

_____

_____

Characters	Plot	Writing	Overall
☆☆☆☆☆	☆☆☆☆☆	☆☆☆☆☆	☆☆☆☆☆

Review _____

_____

_____

_____

_____

_____

_____

_____

_____

_____

_____

_____

_____

Highlights and Quotes _____

_____

_____

_____

_____

_____

_____

_____

Questions _____

_____

_____

_____

_____

_____

_____

Playlist _____

_____

_____

_____

_____

_____

_____

| Book Title and Author or Cover Art | Spice Level 🌶🌶🌶🌶🌶 |

Spice Level 🌶🌶🌶🌶🌶

Format _____

Number of Pages _____

Date Started _____

Date Finished _____

Recommend _____

_____

_____

| Characters | Plot | Writing | Overall |
| ☆☆☆☆☆ | ☆☆☆☆☆ | ☆☆☆☆☆ | ☆☆☆☆☆ |

Review _____

_____

_____

_____

_____

_____

_____

_____

_____

_____

_____

_____

_____

Highlights and Quotes _____

_____

_____

_____

_____

_____

_____

_____

Questions _____

_____

_____

_____

_____

_____

Playlist _____

_____

_____

_____

_____

_____

Book Title and Author or Cover Art	Spice Level 🌶🌶🌶🌶🌶

Format _____

Number of Pages _____

Date Started _____

Date Finished _____

Recommend _____

_____

_____

Characters	Plot	Writing	Overall
☆☆☆☆☆	☆☆☆☆☆	☆☆☆☆☆	☆☆☆☆☆

Review _____

_____

_____

_____

_____

_____

_____

_____

_____

_____

_____

_____

_____

Highlights and Quotes _____

_____

_____

_____

_____

_____

_____

Questions _____

_____

_____

_____

_____

_____

Playlist _____

_____

_____

_____

_____

_____

Book Title and Author or Cover Art	Spice Level 🌶🌶🌶🌶🌶
	Format _____
	Number of Pages _____
	Date Started _____
	Date Finished _____
	Recommend _____
	_____
	_____

Characters	Plot	Writing	Overall
☆☆☆☆☆	☆☆☆☆☆	☆☆☆☆☆	☆☆☆☆☆

Review _____

_____

_____

_____

_____

_____

_____

_____

_____

_____

_____

_____

Highlights and Quotes _____

_____

_____

_____

_____

_____

_____

Questions _____

_____

_____

_____

_____

_____

Playlist _____

_____

_____

_____

_____

_____

Book Title and Author or Cover Art	Spice Level 🌶🌶🌶🌶🌶
	Format _____
	Number of Pages _____
	Date Started _____
	Date Finished _____
	Recommend _____
	_____
	_____

Characters   Plot   Writing   Overall
☆☆☆☆☆   ☆☆☆☆☆   ☆☆☆☆☆   ☆☆☆☆☆

Review _____

_____

_____

_____

_____

_____

_____

_____

_____

_____

_____

_____

Highlights and Quotes _____

_____

_____

_____

_____

_____

_____

Questions _____

_____

_____

_____

_____

_____

Playlist _____

_____

_____

_____

_____

_____

Book Title and Author or Cover Art	Spice Level 🌶🌶🌶🌶🌶
	Format _____
	Number of Pages _____
	Date Started _____
	Date Finished _____
	Recommend _____
	_____
	_____

Characters	Plot	Writing	Overall
☆☆☆☆☆	☆☆☆☆☆	☆☆☆☆☆	☆☆☆☆☆

Review _____

_____

_____

_____

_____

_____

_____

_____

_____

_____

_____

_____

_____

Highlights and Quotes _____

_____

_____

_____

_____

_____

_____

Questions _____

_____

_____

_____

_____

_____

Playlist _____

_____

_____

_____

_____

_____

Book Title and Author or Cover Art	Spice Level 🌶️🌶️🌶️🌶️🌶️
	Format _____
	Number of Pages _____
	Date Started _____
	Date Finished _____
	Recommend _____
	_____
	_____

Characters	Plot	Writing	Overall
☆☆☆☆☆	☆☆☆☆☆	☆☆☆☆☆	☆☆☆☆☆

Review _____

_____

_____

_____

_____

_____

_____

_____

_____

_____

_____

_____

Highlights and Quotes _____

_____

_____

_____

_____

_____

_____

_____

Questions _____

_____

_____

_____

_____

_____

_____

Playlist _____

_____

_____

_____

_____

_____

_____

Book Title and Author or Cover Art	Spice Level 🌶🌶🌶🌶🌶
	Format _____
	Number of Pages _____
	Date Started _____
	Date Finished _____
	Recommend _____
	_____
	_____

Characters	Plot	Writing	Overall
☆☆☆☆☆	☆☆☆☆☆	☆☆☆☆☆	☆☆☆☆☆

Review _____

_____

_____

_____

_____

_____

_____

_____

_____

_____

_____

_____

_____

Highlights and Quotes _____

_____

_____

_____

_____

_____

_____

_____

Questions _____

_____

_____

_____

_____

_____

Playlist _____

_____

_____

_____

_____

_____

Book Title and Author or Cover Art	Spice Level 🌶🌶🌶🌶🌶

Format _____

Number of Pages _____

Date Started _____

Date Finished _____

Recommend _____

_____

_____

Characters	Plot	Writing	Overall
☆☆☆☆☆	☆☆☆☆☆	☆☆☆☆☆	☆☆☆☆☆

Review _____

_____

_____

_____

_____

_____

_____

_____

_____

_____

_____

_____

Highlights and Quotes _____

_____

_____

_____

_____

_____

_____

Questions _____

_____

_____

_____

_____

_____

Playlist _____

_____

_____

_____

_____

_____

Book Title and Author or Cover Art	Spice Level 🌶🌶🌶🌶🌶

Format _____

Number of Pages _____

Date Started _____

Date Finished _____

Recommend _____

_____

_____

Characters	Plot	Writing	Overall
☆☆☆☆☆	☆☆☆☆☆	☆☆☆☆☆	☆☆☆☆☆

Review _____

_____

_____

_____

_____

_____

_____

_____

_____

_____

_____

_____

_____

Highlights and Quotes _____

_____

_____

_____

_____

_____

_____

Questions _____

_____

_____

_____

_____

_____

Playlist _____

_____

_____

_____

_____

_____